Strawberry
Crush
and Other Recipes

Acknowledgments
Executive Editor: Diane Sharpe
Supervising Editor: Stephanie Muller
Design Manager: Sharon Golden
Page Design: Simon Balley Design Associates
Photography: Alex Ramsay

ISBN 0-8114-3774-4

Strawberry
Crush
and Other Recipes

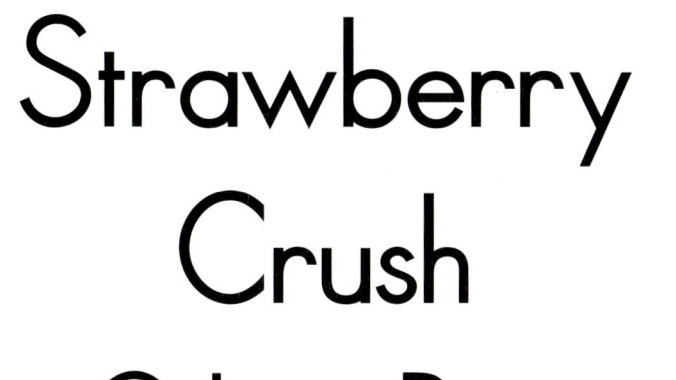

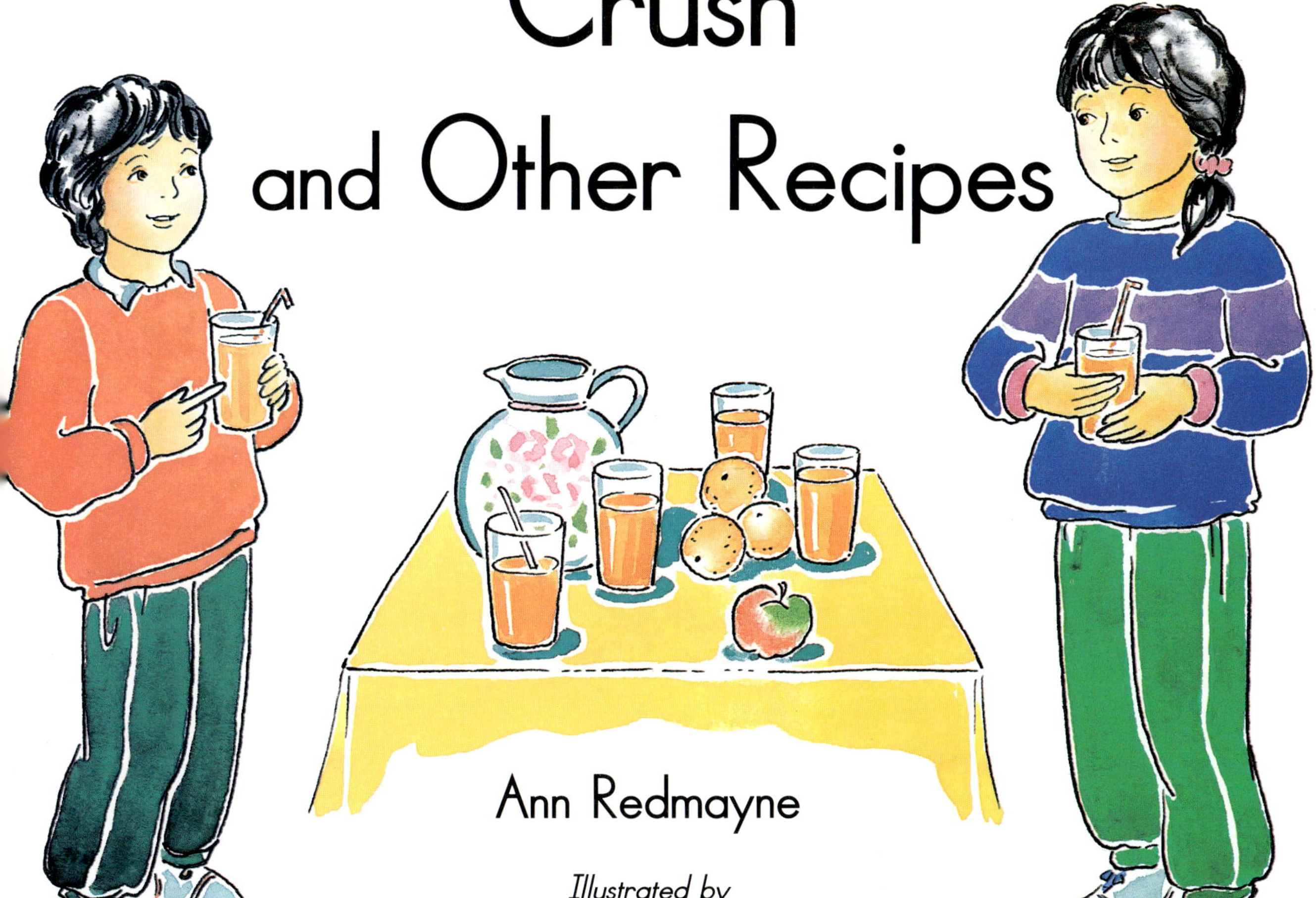

Ann Redmayne

Illustrated by

Kareen Taylerson

STECK-VAUGHN
C O M P A N Y
ELEMENTARY · SECONDARY · ADULT · LIBRARY

These are the drinks we'll make. I'll find the recipes in the cookbook.

Banana Smoothie
Strawberry Crush
Celebration Chocolate
Orange Cloud
Grapefruit Honey Smoothie
Fizzy Fruit Drink

5

It is important to wash your hands
and clean all work areas well before
making food.

BANANA SMOOTHIE

Ingredients

4 bananas

1 quart milk

4 teaspoons brown sugar

Utensils

fork

bowl

teaspoon

measuring cup

spoon

blender

pitcher

Makes enough for one pitcher.

Always ask an adult to work a blender for you. The blades inside one are very sharp.

The blender makes the smoothie nice and frothy.

I'll put the pitcher in the refrigerator now.

Most of the drinks in this book should be put in the refrigerator to cool for two to three hours.

STRAWBERRY CRUSH

Ingredients

1 pint strawberries
1 quart milk

Utensils

colander   cutting board
fork   measuring cup
bowl   blender
knife   pitcher

Makes enough for one pitcher.

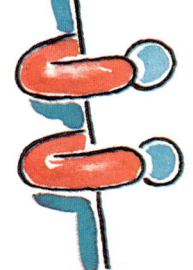

13

If you don't have a garden with strawberries, you can buy fresh or frozen strawberries to use in this recipe.

I've washed the strawberries in the colander and pulled the stems out.

Now I can start mashing them!

14

Save one or two
of the best ones,
and I will slice them.

Mix the milk and strawberries together
in the blender. Then pour it into the
pitcher, and add the strawberry slices.

15

CELEBRATION CHOCOLATE

Ingredients

4 scoops chocolate ice cream
1 quart milk
Chocolate to grate

Utensils

ice cream scoop   small plate
                          4 glasses
grater

Makes enough for four glasses.

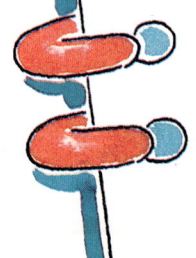

16

I'll put a scoop of chocolate ice cream in the bottom of each glass.

I'll pour in the milk, but I won't stir it. The ice cream will float to the top.

Scooping frozen ice cream out of a container is easier if you wet the spoon first.

I've grated the chocolate for you.

Now I can sprinkle it on top of the drinks.

Don't eat any of that chocolate!

Graters are very sharp. Always ask an adult to grate food for you.

ORANGE CLOUD

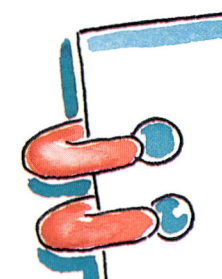

Ingredients

1 quart orange juice
1 cup plain yogurt
1 orange to slice

Utensils

whisk   knife
bowl   cutting board
pitcher

Makes enough for one pitcher.

Yogurt gives this drink a smooth, creamy taste. You can decorate the glasses with the orange slices.

21

GRAPEFRUIT HONEY SMOOTHIE

Ingredients

2 cups milk
2 cups cold grapefruit juice
2 tablespoons honey

Utensils

measuring cup

blender

tablespoon

pitcher

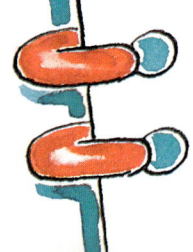

Makes enough for one pitcher.

23

FIZZY FRUIT DRINK

Ingredients

2 cups cold grapefruit juice

2 cups cold apple juice

2 cups cold orange juice

2 cups cold soda water

Strawberries and banana to slice

(Cucumber slices can also be added.)

Utensils

measuring cup   cutting board

large bowl   ladle

knife

Makes enough for 8 glasses.

This drink is Dad's favorite.

Mixing the fruit juices and soda water together is easy.

Now you can float
the fruit slices in the bowl.

26

Mmm, it looks really good.

You should make this Fizzy Fruit Drink right before you are going to drink it. Then it won't lose its fizz.

27

To make the drinks really cool, add ice to them just before serving.

Look, here come the first runners.

Do you remember the names of the drinks the family made? The answers are on the last page, but don't look until you have tried naming everything.

30

1

2

3

4

5

6

Ingredients

apple juice
bananas
brown sugar
chocolate
chocolate ice cream
grapefruit juice
honey

milk
orange
orange juice
soda water
strawberries
yogurt

Utensils

blender
bowls
colander
cutting board
forks
glasses
grater
ice cream scoop
knives

ladle
measuring cups
pitchers
small plate
spoons
tablespoon
teaspoon
whisk

Answers: 1. Banana Smoothie 2. Strawberry Crush 3. Celebration Chocolate
4. Orange Cloud 5. Grapefruit Honey Smoothie 6. Fizzy Fruit Drink